FACING THE FUTURE

DRAMA OF AFRICAN-AMERICAN HISTORY

FACING THE FUTURE

by IRMA McCLAURIN
with VIRGINIA SCHOMP

Marshall Cavendish
Benchmark
New York

For Antonio, Zena, and Denzil . . . my present and my future

The authors and publisher are grateful to Jill Watts, professor of history at California State University, San Marcos, for her perceptive comments on the manuscript, and to the late Richard Newman, civil rights advocate, author, and senior research officer at the W. E. B. DuBois Institute at Harvard University, for his excellent work in formulating the series.

EDITOR: JOYCE STANTON PUBLISHER: MICHELLE BISSON
ART DIRECTOR: ANAHID HAMPARIAN SERIES DESIGNER: MICHAEL NELSON ADDITIONAL RESEARCH: CHIP BIGNESS

MARSHALL CAVENDISH BENCHMARK 99 WHITE PLAINS ROAD TARRYTOWN, NEW YORK 10591-9001
www.marshallcavendish.us Text copyright © 2008 by Irma McClaurin. All rights reserved. No part of this book may be reproduced or utilized in any form or by any means electronic or mechanical, including photocopying, recording, or by any information storage and retrieval system, without permission from the copyright holders. All Internet sites were available and accurate when this book was sent to press.
LIBRARY OF CONGRESS CATALOGING-IN-PUBLICATION DATA: McClaurin, Irma. Facing the future / by Irma McClaurin, with Virginia Schomp. p. cm. — (Drama of African-American history) Summary: "Covers the struggle for racial equality from the end of the civil rights movement in the 1960s to the present day"—Provided by publisher. Includes bibliographical references and index. ISBN 978-0-7614-2644-8
1. African Americans—History—1964—Juvenile literature. 2. African Americans—Social conditions—1975—Juvenile literature. 3. United States—Race relations—Juvenile literature. 4. African Americans—Biography—Juvenile literature. I. Schomp, Virginia. II. Title.
E185.615.M338 2008 973'.0496073—dc22 2007034730

Images provided by Debbie Needleman, Picture Researcher, Portsmouth, NH, from the following sources: Cover and Back cover: Associated Press; page i: Thinking, 1990 (oil on board) by Carlton Murrell (Contemporary Artist), Private Collection/ The Bridgeman Art Library; pages ii-iii, 6, 10, 16 top and bottom, 18, 20, 22, 29, 30, 37, 39, 42, 43, 47, 48, 52, 58, 65: Associated Press; pages. 8, 13, 38: Time Life Pictures/Getty Images; page 9: Youth Radio; page 21: Courtesy Chicago Defender; page 24: Joseph Schwartz/CORBIS; page 26: Charles O'Rear/CORBIS; page 27: Ralf-Finn Hestoft/CORBIS; page 32: Chip East/Reuters/CORBIS; pages 34, 40: Bettmann/CORBIS; page 44: LEE CELANO/AFP/Getty Images; page 46: Underwood & Underwood/CORBIS; page 50: Art Resource, NY; page 51, 53: Getty Images; page 54, 56: NBAE/Getty Images; page 55: Tony Duffy/Allsport/Getty Images; page 61: Landall Kyle Carter/Reuters/CORBIS; page 62: Andrew Lichtenstein/CORBIS; page 64: Mark Peterson/CORBIS; page 67: Annie Griffiths Belt/CORBIS; page 68: The Smiley Group/Kevin Foley/KCET; page 71: Smiley N. Pool/Dallas Morning News/CORBIS

Printed in China
1 3 5 6 4 2

Front cover: Author, publisher, and entrepreneur Earl Graves
Back cover: High school students perform at the 2004 Hip-Hop Summit in Syracuse, New York.
Half-title page: *Thinking* by Caribbean-born artist Carlton Murrell
Title page: Students in a fourth-grade reading class in New York City

CONTENTS

Novelist Alice Walker achieved fame and a Pulitzer Prize for her powerful book *The Color Purple.*

INTRODUCTION

Facing the Future is the tenth and final volume in the series Drama of African-American History. Earlier books in this series have taken us all the way from the start of the transatlantic slave trade in the fifteenth century through the civil rights movement of the 1950s and 1960s. Along the way we have met a host of fascinating figures. We traveled with Olaudah Equiano on a slave ship from West Africa to colonial America in the mid-1700s. We watched Nat Turner lead a slave uprising in nineteenth-century Virginia. We joined Frederick Douglass and Sojourner Truth in their Civil War–era battles against slavery. During the Reconstruction period and the "Jim Crow" era, we saw African Americans confront racial oppression and violence. During the modern civil rights movement, we witnessed the courage and determination of Martin Luther King Jr., Malcolm X, and other black leaders. Now we will meet a new generation of freedom fighters: the black men, women, and children who have carried on the struggle for racial equality from the end of the civil rights movement through the present day.

Hundreds of thousands of African Americans joined forces in the civil rights movement. By the mid-1960s, they had achieved many impressive gains. The Jim Crow laws stripping black Americans of their civil and political rights had been overturned. New laws had been passed guaranteeing African Americans equal access to public facilities and equal opportunities in employment and education. The number of registered black voters in the South had soared, leading to record numbers of black elected officials.

The leaders of the civil rights movement viewed these achievements with pride. At the same time, they knew that the fight for freedom was far from won. Poverty and unemployment rates remained far higher among black Americans than whites. Racial discrimination persisted in many areas of American society. Moderate and more radical leaders disagreed over the best way to tackle these serious problems. Their conflicts gradually began to divide the once strong and unified civil rights movement. The assassination of Martin Luther King Jr. in April 1968 completed the unraveling. With the loss of its most influential leader, the movement split into a number of separate groups, each with its own strategies and goals.

The decades that followed would bring both disappointments and triumphs. A nationwide economic downturn would hit black families much harder than whites. A growing mood of conservatism in white America would erode some of the hard-won gains of the civil rights movement. Despite these setbacks, African Americans continued to strive toward Martin Luther King's dream of racial equal-

A protester demands an end to racism at the 1995 Million Man March in Washington, D.C.

FACING THE FUTURE

ity. In 1986 they reflected on their history and heritage in the first national observance of Martin Luther King Jr. Day. In 1995 they renewed their commitment to serving and strengthening the black community at the Million Man March. That historic event brought tens of thousands of African-American men and boys to Washington, D.C. Twelve-year-old Anyi Howell was thrilled as he watched the celebration

Award-winning radio reporter Anyi Howell explores social issues affecting the black community.

of "unity, atonement, and brotherhood" on television. Ten years later, Anyi attended the Millions More Movement's anniversary march and came away with "the sense that a radical change is in the near future."

Today young freedom fighters like Anyi Howell gain strength and confidence from their ancestors in the four-hundred-year struggle for African-American rights. Frederick Douglass foresaw their continuing labors when he wrote, "If there is no struggle, there is no progress. . . . Power concedes nothing without a demand. It never did, and it never will." Recently African-American educator Howard L. Fuller echoed that declaration. "We have known deep rivers of sorrows," said Fuller, "and we have experienced vast deserts of despair but somehow, some way, we have persevered. . . . Cast away illusions and prepare for struggle. I say: 'It must be a struggle!'"

President Bill Clinton presents the Congressional Gold Medal to Elizabeth Eckford of the Little Rock Nine.

Chapter 1

The Crisis in Education

In September 1997 President Bill Clinton opened the front doors of a school in Little Rock, Arkansas, to nine middle-aged men and women. Forty years earlier, the group known as the Little Rock Nine* had endured a firestorm of racial hatred when they tried to enter Central High School. An angry white mob had threatened to lynch them. Arkansas governor Orval Faubus had called out the National Guard to prevent them from integrating the all-white school. In the end President Dwight Eisenhower had been forced to send in armed paratroopers to escort the students to class. Reflecting on the fortieth anniversary of those historic events, President Clinton declared, "What happened here changed the course of our country forever. . . . For, surely it was here at Central High that we took another giant step closer to the idea of America."

*For more on the Little Rock Nine, see volume 9 in this series, *The Civil Rights Movement.*

In 1999 the Little Rock Nine were honored with the nation's highest civilian award, the Congressional Gold Medal. Speaking for the group, Ernest Green recalled the long journey from the jeers and threats of 1957 to the awards ceremony. "I think each of us would consider it worthwhile," he said. "While the sacrifices have been great, we recognized in 1957 that it was not an easy journey." Green also shared the group's greatest hope: that the story of their commitment and triumph would teach today's young people that they have the "opportunity to change their life and their destiny."

LEVELING THE PLAYING FIELD

The ordeals of the Little Rock Nine grew out of the 1954 Supreme Court decision in the case of *Brown* v. *Board of Education*. In that landmark ruling, the Court had declared that school segregation was unconstitutional. The ruling had outraged white segregationists across the South, where Jim Crow laws required the separation of the races in practically every area of public life. Southern state governments and local school boards had responded with a variety of tactics to delay school integration. Even the victory in Little Rock was short-lived. A year after the Little Rock Nine enrolled at Central High, Governor Faubus closed all of the city's high schools rather than proceed with desegregation.

A decade after the *Brown* decision, less than 2 percent of African-American students in the South were attending integrated schools. Then President Lyndon Johnson signed the Civil Rights Act of 1964 into law. The new law specifically prohibited discrimination in education and other areas. It gave the federal government the power to enforce desegregation. In a series of important rulings, federal courts ordered southern school districts to end their delaying tactics. By 1968, 32 percent of southern black students were attending integrated schools. Four years later, that figure had climbed to 45 percent.

One of the main methods used to achieve school integration was busing. Blacks and whites generally lived in segregated neighborhoods in the South, which automatically meant that they attended separate schools. To correct that racial imbalance, the courts ordered school districts to bus some black students to all-white schools and some white students to all-black schools. Critics argued that court-ordered busing violated the rights of communities to control their own schools. The protests went all the way to the Supreme Court. In 1971 the Court upheld the use of busing to achieve school integration. That decision had far-reaching consequences not only in the South but throughout the nation. Most northern states had outlawed school segregation a century earlier. However, racial prejudice and discrimination still restricted most northern blacks to segregated city ghettos and "colored schools." Now northern school districts would have to improve educational opportunities for black students by developing busing plans.

Police escort a line of buses through the streets of South Boston in 1974 in an effort to achieve school integration.

Another new civil rights program that changed the face of American education was affirmative action. In 1965 President Johnson argued that ensuring equal opportunities for African Americans required more than simply prohibiting discrimination. Positive or "affirmative" actions also must be taken to "level the playing field" and give a boost to people who had been held back by centuries of racial injustice. "We seek not just freedom but opportunity," Johnson explained. "We seek . . . not just equality as a right and a theory, but equality as a fact and as a result."

Under federal affirmative action guidelines, colleges and universities were required to develop programs to increase their proportion of minority students. (The program was later extended to cover discrimination against women, too.) Sometimes affirmative action meant making extra efforts to recruit blacks, Hispanics, and other minorities. Schools also might take race into account in decisions about admissions. For example, admissions officers might apply lower standards to black applicants than whites, or they might set aside a certain number of seats for minorities.

THE CONSERVATIVE BACKLASH

School desegregation programs produced a number of positive results. Many minority children were able to get a better education at schools formerly restricted to whites. That improved their chances for going to college and finding good jobs. Integration also improved relations between children of different races. One study of city schools in Kentucky showed that more than 90 percent of high school students, both black and white, were comfortable working with students of other races and learning about each other's cultures.

There were also some unexpected negatives. First, many black schools were closed when all-white public schools were desegregated. That took a toll on black communities. In addition, many white parents moved to suburban areas or placed their children in private schools rather than send them to integrated city schools. "White flight" would gradually lead to the nearly complete "resegregation" of newly integrated school systems in Atlanta, Georgia; Richmond, Virginia; Boston, Massachusetts; and other cities. Finally, there were some problems when whites and blacks attended the same schools. Teachers and administrators often discriminated against black children in integrated schools, sometimes in well-meaning ways. For example, they might steer black students toward less challenging courses and hold them to lower academic standards than whites. Racial tensions between white and black students also led to arguments and occasionally to violence.

The mid-1970s brought a growing white backlash against affirmative action and other civil rights programs. The conflict over affirmative action came to a head in the case of *University of California Regents* v. *Bakke.* Allan Bakke was a young white man who had been twice rejected for admission to the medical school at the University of California at Davis. Under the university's affirmative action policies, sixteen seats were set aside for minority students each year. Some of the minority students who were admitted instead of Bakke had lower grades and test scores than he did. That was "reverse discrimination," Bakke argued, because it favored minorities over whites. The case reached the Supreme Court in 1978. The justices were divided in their opinions. In the end they issued what many viewed as a

A conservative students' group at Roger Williams University in Bristol, Rhode Island, presents a "whites-only" scholarship, created as a protest against affirmative action.

Students at the University of Michigan celebrate a 2003 Supreme Court decision upholding the affirmative action policies of the university's law school.

confusing and contradictory decision, saying that colleges could take race into account in admissions but that setting fixed numbers, or "quotas," for minorities was unconstitutional.

The conservative backlash continued to grow in the 1980s and 1990s. Well-organized campaigns against affirmative action were mounted in several states. In California and Washington, voters passed measures ending the affirmative action programs that had helped integrate their state universities. Meanwhile, school busing came under increasingly determined attacks. In Boston white parents sued the school board in 1999, charging that their children had been denied entrance to particular schools because of their race. As a result of that lawsuit, Boston ended its twenty-five-year program of busing and dropped race as a factor in deciding which schools children could attend. A number of other cities across the country saw similar lawsuits. In some cases conservative courts ordered an end not only to busing but also to all other special efforts to integrate schools. That contributed to resegregation and the return of an unequal school system.

A Report Card on Education

Today a report card on education would have to give America's schools an "incomplete" in their progress toward providing equal opportunities to all children, regardless of race. The state of education for African Americans is clearly better than it was fifty years ago. Jim Crow laws no longer bar black students from the better schools in the South. Mobs no longer threaten violence when blacks enroll in historically white schools. Dedicated teachers in school districts across the country work hard to make sure every child has the chance for a quality education.

At the same time, the promise of the Supreme Court's *Brown* decision remains largely unfulfilled. According to a recent study by the Civil Rights Project at Harvard University, only about 50 percent of black students graduate from high school, compared to 75 percent of whites. A 2005 report by the National Assessment of Educational Progress showed that white and Asian children had higher average scores than black children in reading and math.

Researchers point to several possible reasons for this achievement gap. African-American and Hispanic students are far more likely than white students to attend schools in high-poverty areas. These high-minority schools are nearly always overcrowded and underfunded. They do not have the resources to provide students with adequate supplies, the latest technology, and experienced teachers. Studies have also shown that many teachers do not encourage minority students to work hard and take challenging courses. In addition, poverty and the lingering effects of past discrimination can limit a child's educational opportunities.

The No Child Left Behind Act (NCLB) was intended to fix

Under No Child Left Behind, this New York City schoolgirl will take state tests on math and reading each year from grades three to eight.

those problems. Signed into law by President George W. Bush in 2002, NCLB set ambitious goals for improving education. It mandated extensive testing of public school students and imposed strict penalties on schools whose scores fall below achievement goals. Supporters argue that No Child Left Behind has succeeded in shining a spotlight on failing schools. Critics point out that in some ways the law has created more problems than solutions for poor and minority students. Some states have lowered their overall achievement standards in order to help students pass their tests and help schools avoid federal penalties. Teachers have sometimes focused on boosting the test scores of average students while ignoring those who test below grade level. No Child Left Behind has also failed to provide struggling schools with the funds needed to hire qualified teachers and give them the tools they need to succeed at their jobs.

Another area of continuing controversy in public education has been the use of race as a factor in school admissions. In 2007 the Supreme Court addressed the debate with its ruling in the case of *Parents Involved in Community Schools* v. *Seattle School District*. A group of white parents in Seattle had sued their school district after their children were refused admission to the schools of their choice because of their race. The school district's programs were designed to promote integration by considering race when deciding whether a student should be allowed to enroll in a particular school. In a 5-4 decision, the

Supreme Court declared that such programs were unconstitutional. Public schools could not try to achieve racial diversity through programs based solely on a student's race. The ruling did not forbid school districts from encouraging integration through other means, however, such as considering family income in admissions decisions.

Critics argued that the *Seattle School District* ruling violated the principles of the 1954 *Brown* v. *Board of Education* ruling. Hundreds of school districts across the country scrambled to figure out whether the new ruling meant that they would have to change their race-based admissions policies. It is too early to tell how the Court's actions will affect future efforts at school integration. But one thing seems certain: Americans remain bitterly divided over the role of race in America's schools and the best way to provide a quality education to all children.

LOOKING TO THE FUTURE

Many ideas have been proposed for closing the achievement gap between white and minority students. Supporters of affirmative action programs argue that such measures are still needed to combat the effects of past discrimination. Black communities have fought for greater control of their schools. Local control would give parents the authority to replace teachers, principals, and teaching methods that are not meeting their children's needs.

A number of concerned individuals and groups have developed alternative educational systems to empower families and increase educational opportunities for minority children. The National Association of Street Schools developed a nationwide network of schools that provide personalized education to at-risk youth. The See Forever Foundation offers academic and

Educator and civil rights activist Robert Moses developed the Algebra Project to bring crucial math skills to young people in poor communities.

job-training programs to teenagers in lower-income communities. The Algebra Project, created by civil rights veteran Robert Moses, gives inner-city and rural students the math skills needed to compete in the twenty-first century. Benjamin Banneker Academic High School in Washington, D.C., offers a rigorous academic program that prepares urban students for admission to the nation's best colleges and universities. Another alternative school in Washington, the Duke Ellington School of the Arts, nurtures a passion for the arts in talented youngsters who might not otherwise have a chance to develop their artistic skills.

In 2000, Dr. Howard L. Fuller founded the Black Alliance for Educational Options to encourage the development of alternative programs such as these. Fuller argues that more students will succeed if families are able to choose among a variety of effective educational options. These might include charter schools (public schools that operate independently of local school boards), public-private partnerships, homeschooling, cyberschools, black independent schools, and other options. "We must give poor parents the power to choose schools— public or private, nonsectarian [not associated with a religious group] or religious—where their children will succeed," says Fuller. "And we must give all schools the incentives to value children and work to meet their needs."

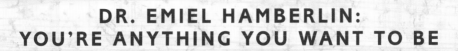

DR. EMIEL HAMBERLIN:
YOU'RE ANYTHING YOU WANT TO BE

Imagine a class in which today's assignment includes feeding the alligator and teaching speech to the macaws. Dr. Emiel Hamberlin imagined that and much more. When Hamberlin became a substitute teacher at Chicago's DuSable High School in 1964, he was just filling time before starting his planned career with the Peace Corps. He soon discovered that teaching was his true calling. In more than forty years of working with inner-city schoolchildren, this inspiring science teacher has strived to "change

Students in Emiel Hamberlin's science classes enjoy close encounters with raccoons, snakes, salamanders, and other animals.

lives and mend broken spirits through the power of education." Most of his students come from a failed housing project marked by poverty, crime, drugs, and gang violence. Hamberlin's mission is to remind them that they are wonderful, original individuals with the power to change their lives and become anything they want to be. "I want students to know that I care what they do with their lives," he explains. "My fellow teachers and I put success on their minds, and then push, shake, cajole, shout and sometimes even force success into them."

Hamberlin believes in surrounding his students with their subject matter. His classroom is filled with plants and animals. Students care for tropical plants and maintain habitats for peacocks, pheasants, and other exotic animals at an indoor-outdoor laboratory on the school campus. Hamberlin's classes have also developed a number of small business enterprises, including a profitable landscaping club that has beautified public housing complexes and transformed vacant lots into community gardens.

In 2001 Emiel Hamberlin was inducted into the National Teachers Hall of Fame. His greatest reward, however, has been the former students who return to his classroom nearly every day to tell him that he made a positive impact on their lives. "He spent countless hours telling [us] what great things we would be doing and how much we were needed," said one graduate. "He believed in me and my classmates when we did not believe in ourselves."

Chapter 2

THE ECONOMIC DIVIDE

Earl Graves grew up in Brooklyn, New York, in the Jim Crow era. His family lived in Bedford-Stuyvesant, a vibrant neighborhood comprised mainly of hardworking black homeowners. That environment inspired Graves with "the idea of wanting to do something of my own." After graduating from college, he worked in politics and business. Then, in 1970, he founded Black Enterprise *magazine. The civil rights movement had encouraged African Americans to build self-reliance and economic independence by establishing their own businesses. Graves wanted to give black business owners the knowledge they would need to succeed in a white-dominated world.*

Black Enterprise *has been a phenomenal success. In 2001 it entered its fourth decade with 4 million readers and $5.7 million in sales. Graves has used his magazine not only to help black businesspeople achieve their goals but also to speak out on civil rights*

Opposite: Earl Graves poses with his best-selling book *How to Succeed in Business without Being White.*

issues. One of his main messages is that African Americans must "come together . . . to defend and protect the gains we have made and to make sure that we all continue to move forward. . . . We have to form a united front of all Black men, women and children and work toward true equality—economic equality."

THE POSTWAR BOOM

When Earl Graves founded *Black Enterprise* in 1970, the United States was in the midst of an economic boom. Workers' wages had climbed steadily since the end of World War II twenty-five years earlier. Hundreds of thousands of American families had risen from poverty to join the growing middle class. The economic status of black Americans had improved along with the rest of society. The African-American poverty rate had fallen, and a thriving new black middle class had emerged. More black people than ever before were buying their

Children ride their tricycles in Brooklyn, New York, during the post–World War II economic boom.

FACING THE FUTURE

own homes and starting their own businesses.

The economic gains made by African Americans were due not only to the booming economy but also to the civil rights laws that had helped pave the way for black advancement. The most important of these laws was the Civil Rights Act of 1964. Earlier in this book, we learned about the impact of that groundbreaking legislation on school segregation. The Civil Rights Act also prohibited discrimination in employment. Under its provisions, affirmative action programs were designed to improve economic opportunities for African Americans. Government agencies and private employers worked toward racial diversity in the workplace by making extra efforts to recruit and hire black and other minority job applicants.

A 1971 Supreme Court ruling broadened the scope of affirmative action in employment. In the case of *Griggs* v. *Duke Power Co.*, the Court ruled that hiring policies that tended to exclude minorities were illegal even if the company did not intend to discriminate. For example, a policy requiring job applicants to have a high school diploma would automatically favor whites. That was legal only if the employer could prove that the workers' duties actually required a high school education.

Despite the benefits of affirmative action, African Americans were still far from achieving full economic equality. In 1970 the black poverty rate was more than two and a half times higher than the national rate. The average black family's income was only about 61 percent of a white family's. African-American economist Julianne Malveaux explained the inequalities this way: "When it is cold in the overall economy, black America finds itself freezing. And when the overall economy experiences a sunny day, somehow black folks are located under a cloud."

THE NEW CONSERVATISM

In the mid-1970s America's long period of postwar growth and prosperity came to an end. The nation's unemployment rates began to climb. So did poverty rates. As always, the economic downturn hit black Americans harder than whites. In the late 1970s and 1980s, blacks were at least twice as likely as whites to be unemployed. The percentage of African Americans living in poverty climbed to about three to four times the white poverty rate.

The conservative backlash made the hard times even harder. Beginning in the late 1970s, affirmative action in the workplace came under increasing attack from opponents who charged that hiring preferences for minorities were "reverse discrimination." Ronald Reagan, president from 1981 to 1989, threw the weight of the federal government behind those complaints. Under the Reagan administration, the Department of Justice placed restrictions on affirmative action in hiring by federal contractors. The department also filed lawsuits against affirmative action programs that had increased the numbers of black police officers and firefighters in Detroit, Boston, and other cities. In

Cuts in social service programs such as food stamps meant increased hardships for poor families during the conservative backlash of the 1980s and early 1990s.

addition, Reagan made numerous cuts in social services to the poor, including food stamps, the Aid to Families with Dependent Children program, and training and public employment programs.

In 1989 President George H. W. Bush took office. Like Reagan, Bush was a conservative Republican who favored limits on social services and affirmative action. In 1992 he lost his reelection bid to the Democratic candidate, Bill Clinton. The economy improved under President Clinton, lifting African Americans along with the rest of society. The average black family's income grew by 33 percent, while black unemployment fell to near-record lows. A conservative mood continued to dominate the nation, however. A 1995 *Washington Post* poll showed that three out of four Americans believed that hiring preferences for minorities were unnecessary and unfair. The response of one white store owner from South Carolina was typical: "The blacks think we owe something for going getting them [from Africa]. I didn't go get anybody. That was 200 years ago. Why should I suffer so they can have a better chance in jobs or anything for that matter?"

A volunteer helps a little girl open a box of cereal at a church-run nutrition program in Chicago.

The continuing conservative climate helped put George W. Bush in the White House in 2001. President Bush's economic policies centered on long-term tax cuts for the wealthiest Americans. The cost of the tax cuts was often balanced with cutbacks in programs benefiting poor and working-class families. According to Gene Sperling, director of economic programs at

the Center for American Progress, the result was "a triple-burn for African Americans." Under the Bush administration, wrote Sperling, blacks experienced a sharp rise in unemployment, "received the least from the most expensive tax cuts in history," and suffered from the "squeeze" on funding for "education, healthcare, public housing, job training, small business development, and other areas vital to students, working families and entrepreneurs."

RACE AND WEALTH

Today the economic landscape for black Americans is filled with contradictions. Forty years after the end of the civil rights movement, the black middle class is larger than ever. Civil rights legislation has given millions of African Americans access to higher-paying jobs once restricted to whites. In 2006 the nation had more than 4 million black-owned and operated businesses, generating nearly $7 billion in annual earnings.

At the same time, African Americans are twice as likely as whites to be unemployed. Black workers still earn less than whites, even in top professions. One recent study found that black lawyers, doctors, and dentists make about eighty cents for every dollar earned by their white counterparts. Comparisons of wealth (how much people *own* rather than what they *earn*) sharply illustrate the racial inequalities. In 2003, reported black educator Melvin Oliver, African Americans had "only eight cents for every dollar of wealth that White Americans possess. Class status does not erase this striking difference, as even middle-class Blacks have substantially less wealth than their White counterparts."

There are many reasons behind this continuing economic

divide. Older generations of African Americans who toiled under the Jim Crow system built up less wealth than whites. As a result, their children and grandchildren have not inherited the extra funds that could help them get through hard times and invest in new opportunities. Past discrimination also has left many African Americans without the education and skills needed to succeed in an increasingly complex, high-tech economy.

Harlem business-woman Sylvia Woods celebrates the fortieth anniversary of her black-owned and operated restaurant.

Continuing discrimination adds to African Americans' economic burdens. Studies have shown that minorities have a harder time finding jobs than whites. In one survey conducted by the University of Chicago and the Massachusetts Institute of Technology, researchers sent out thousands of fake resumés in response to employment ads. About one out of ten resumés with "white-sounding" names generated phone calls from prospective employers. Only one in fifteen resumés with names popular among African Americans received calls.

African Americans also face discrimination from banks and other financial institutions. According to recent studies, banks are at least twice as likely to reject black applicants for home loans as whites. Rejected black applicants often turn to finance companies that specialize in loans to low-income borrowers in minority communities. These small, unregulated lenders typically charge sky-high interest rates. A 1993 *Chicago Tribune* article described the plight of some 20,000 low-income homeowners in Georgia who borrowed from one shady firm. Unable to pay the excessive interest on their loans, many of the black families ended up losing their homes. "This is a system of segregation, really," said one attorney. "We don't have separate water fountains [anymore], but we have separate lending institutions."

THE CONTINUING FIGHT

How should America address the continuing economic divide between black and white citizens? Many people have called for stricter enforcement of existing antidiscrimination laws. Some have argued that affirmative action programs are still needed to overcome the effects of past discrimination and promote racial diversity in the workplace. Other proposals have included programs to help minorities get job training, go to college, buy homes, and start businesses. In addition, a social movement within the black community has called for "racial reparations." These payments would repay the descendants of African slaves for the social and economic injuries inflicted by centuries of oppression.

Earl Graves, founder of *Black Enterprise* magazine, points

OPRAH WINFREY: "YOU CAN GET THERE"

When Oprah Winfrey was growing up in rural Mississippi, no one could have predicted that the impoverished little girl would one day become one of the wealthiest and most admired women in the world. Oprah was raised by her stern, demanding grandmother until the age of six. Then she was sent up north to live with a mother she barely knew. Her home environment was chaotic and abusive. When the teenager responded by acting out, she was packed off to her father in Nashville, Tennessee. Under his strict but loving discipline, Oprah blossomed. She worked hard at school, excelling in the drama and public-speaking clubs. She even entered and won her first beauty pageant. Most importantly, she discovered within herself a strong drive to succeed and the firm belief that "whatever your goal, you can get there if you're willing to work."

Oprah Winfrey is named Favorite Talk Show Host at the 2004 People's Choice Awards.

Oprah began her broadcasting career while she was still in high school, working as a newscaster at a local radio station. At age nineteen she became the first black woman news anchor at Nashville's WTVF-TV. In 1984 she moved to Chicago to host a TV talk show. Within two years, *The Oprah Winfrey Show* was reaching a nationwide audience. Oprah's uplifting stories, her warm and personal style, and her ability to connect with ordinary women made her program the highest-rated talk show in television history. *The Oprah Winfrey Show* would remain America's number-one daytime talk show for more than twenty years. It would also make its superstar host a fortune. By age thirty-two, Oprah was a millionaire. At fifty, she joined the exclusive ranks of the world's billionaires.

Oprah Winfrey's entrepreneurial spirit has taken her media empire beyond television into areas including a film company, a monthly magazine, and the world's largest book club. She has also used her great wealth to support a number of public and private charities. Her latest project is the Oprah Winfrey Leadership Academy for Girls in South Africa. Opened in 2007, this state-of-the-art school offers a first-class education to promising young girls from impoverished backgrounds. "I believe that my own success has come from a love of learning," Oprah explains. "I wanted to build a safe place where these growing young women could live and learn. . . . I wanted them to feel inspired, to honor their individual callings. I wanted them to literally dwell in possibility."

RUSSELL SIMMONS: "EVERYTHING YOU NEED TO KNOW ABOUT SUCCESS IS INSIDE OF YOU"

As a teenager in a lower-middle-class neighborhood in Queens, New York, Russell Simmons flirted with drugs and gang life. Then he heard rap music. In the mid-1970s this fresh new form of music was just emerging from New York's African-American communities. Rap offered young urban blacks a chance to express themselves freely, without set rules or expensive equipment. Unlike mainstream black performers who sought success by conforming to white America's expectations, rappers "kept it real." They remained true to the whole hip-hop culture, which includes not only rap music but also the language, style of dress, and mind-set of the streets. Gradually, hip-hop's appeal spread to a wider audience, including hordes of record-buying white suburban youths. At the center of this phenomenal growth was Russell Simmons.

Russell Simmons sees today's black youths as future entrepreneurs who "will make a difference economically in our community."

Simmons began organizing hip-hop parties and concerts while he was a student at City College in New York. His success led him to record producing. In 1983 he helped form Run-DMC, the first hip-hop group with "crossover" appeal (meaning that it was as popular with whites as blacks.) A year later, he and partner Rick Rubin founded Def Jam Recordings. Simmons signed a number of unknowns to his new label, including soon-to-be-famous artists such as Public Enemy, Kurtis Blow, and LL Cool J. Later, the tireless promoter branched out into a hip-hop clothing line, an advertising agency, and the cable TV programs *Def Comedy Jam* and *Def Poetry Jam.* In recent years he has also devoted his energies to political and social causes, including projects to encourage education, political involvement, and the empowerment of black youth.

Simmons credits his success to the entrepreneurial spirit that kept him going despite all the obstacles and criticisms along the way. "You have to stick with what you start," he says. "Everything you need to know about success is inside of you, because I believe it is inside of all of us.

out that many important changes have taken place to open the doors for African-American achievement. "It is important to remind ourselves from time to time that the . . . economic strides and accomplishments that fill the pages of BE each month were unimaginable just a few short decades ago," he wrote in a 2000 editorial titled "A Letter to My Grandchildren." Graves also reminded young readers that there is still a great deal of work to be done:

> As committed a champion as I am of success, the fact is that its trappings and its hype have distracted us from our higher purpose: the fight for true equal opportunity for all Americans. As a result, we are losing some of the ground that the previous generation fought for and gained for our benefit—and for your benefit. . . . Your parents are doing what they can to continue the battle in their generation. I hope you will lead the charge in your generation, as I have no reason to believe it will have yet been won.

Chapter 3

POLITICAL POWER

In 1965 President Lyndon Johnson signed the Voting Rights Act. The new law, which banned the discriminatory requirements that had denied southern blacks their voting rights, was one of the greatest victories of the civil rights movement. Armed with the vote, African Americans would throw hundreds of racist sheriffs, mayors, and other government officials out of office.

Key provisions of the Voting Rights Act were set to expire in August 2007. In 2006 Congress took up the question of whether to reauthorize the act. A group of southern Republican lawmakers opposed renewal, arguing that some of the act's provisions were no longer fair or necessary. A coalition made up of more than one hundred civil rights groups and their allies disagreed. In the days leading up to the congressional vote, the coalition held rallies in communities across the nation. Volunteers collected more than 100,000 petitions. Voters flooded congressional offices with so many phone calls that one senator's phones were shut down with the sheer volume of calls.

Opposite: Shirley Chisholm flashes a victory sign after winning the 1968 congressional election in the Twelfth District of Brooklyn, New York.

The massive effort paid off. In July 2006 the Senate voted unanimously to extend the Voting Rights Act for another twenty-five years. African-American author and political commentator Tavis Smiley hailed the victory as evidence of what black Americans can achieve when they work together for a common cause. "A profound lesson was learned from this process," wrote Smiley, "and must be applied to all of our struggles: The power of a single individual, when combined with many, creates a mighty force."

IN THE HALLS OF POWER

The Voting Rights Act of 1965 and other achievements of the civil rights movement led to dramatic advances for African Americans in the political arena. Voter registration among blacks in the lower South increased from 21 percent in 1962 to more than 60 percent in 1967. As the number of black voters increased, so did the number of African Americans elected to office. In 1964 there were about five hundred black elected officials in the nation. By 2000, the total exceeded nine thousand.

In the past half century, African Americans have served at nearly every level of government. Black mayors have been elected in most major cities, including Atlanta, Georgia; Chicago, Illinois; Detroit, Michigan; Los Angeles, California; Memphis, Tennessee; Newark, New Jersey; New York City; and Washington, D.C. In 1989 Virginia elected the nation's first black governor, L. Douglas Wilder. About twenty years earlier, Shirley Chisholm of New York had become the first black woman elected to Congress. Other prominent African Americans in Congress have included Representatives John Conyers of Michigan, Harold Ford Jr. of Tennessee, Barbara Jordan of Texas, John Lewis of Georgia, Charles Rangel of New York, and

Andrew Young of Georgia, as well as Senators Carol Moseley Braun and Barack Obama, both of Illinois. Today more than forty African-American representatives and senators belong to the Congressional Black Caucus, an organization formed in 1969 to "promote the public welfare through legislation designed to meet the needs of millions of neglected citizens."

Black Americans have also made substantial inroads in non-elective government offices. Secretary of Housing and Urban Development Robert C. Weaver was the first African American to serve in a presidential cabinet. Andrew Young was the United States' first black ambassador to the United Nations. In 1967 Thurgood Marshall, the great-grandson of a slave, became the first African-American justice of the U.S. Supreme Court. Twenty-four years later, President George H. W. Bush nominated Clarence Thomas to serve as the second black Supreme Court justice.

Former senator Carol Moseley Braun of Illinois addresses delegates at the 2004 Democratic National Convention.

The Clinton administration marked the first time African Americans served at the top levels of government in numbers reflecting their population in the United States. During his two terms, President Clinton appointed seven black cabinet secretaries and nominated more black federal judges than in the previous sixteen years combined. President George W. Bush matched Clinton's record, appointing a number of African Americans and Hispanics to top government posts. Under Bush, General Colin Powell became the first African-American secretary of state. Powell was followed in that office by Condoleezza Rice.

Robert C. Weaver served as secretary of the Department of Housing and Urban Development under President Lyndon Johnson.

REACHING FOR THE TOP

Practically the only level of government that African Americans haven't cracked yet is the presidency. In 1972 Rep. Shirley Chisholm became the first woman and the first African American to run a major nationwide campaign for the White House. (A few other women and blacks had run previously on minor party tickets.) Chisholm won 152 delegates before withdrawing from the race. She later wrote that she ran for the presidency "because someone had to do it first. . . . The next time a woman runs, or a black, a Jew or anyone from a group that the country is 'not ready' to elect to its highest office, I believe he or she will be taken seriously from the start."

The Reverend Jesse Jackson made two Democratic presidential

CONDOLEEZZA RICE: "TWICE AS GOOD"

On a Sunday morning in September 1963, eight-year-old Condoleezza Rice felt the floor shake in the Birmingham, Alabama, church where she sat worshipping with her parents. Two miles away, white segregationists had bombed the Sixteenth Street Baptist Church, killing four young black girls. A few days later, Condi attended the funeral of one of her classmates. "I remember more than anything the coffins," she later said. "The small coffins. And the sense that Birmingham wasn't a very safe place."

In the 1960s Birmingham was widely considered the most segregated city in the South. Condi Rice's childhood, however, was shaped more by the expectations of her parents than the harsh realities of racial discrimination. The Rices dedicated themselves to their young daughter's education. They filled Condi's days with lessons in piano, ballet, violin, figure skating, speed reading, and French. They taught her that she would have to be "twice as good" as a white person to succeed in the Jim Crow world.

Condoleezza Rice has visited more than sixty-five countries in her role as U.S. secretary of state.

The message took root. Condi Rice was an exceptional student who graduated from high school at age fifteen. After completing her studies at the University of Denver, she taught political science at Stanford University. Her talents brought her to the attention of President George H. W. Bush, who named her special assistant for national security affairs. In 1999 Rice advised the president's son, George W. Bush, during his presidential campaign. After the younger Bush was elected, he appointed Rice to the position of national security adviser. Later, she succeeded Colin Powell to become the first black female secretary of state.

Condoleezza Rice has been criticized for her role as spokesperson for President Bush's foreign policy, especially regarding the 2003 invasion of Iraq. Some African-American commentators have also questioned her conservative worldview, which one columnist called "so radically different from that of most black Americans." Rice answers her critics with the same blend of strength and confidence that made the little girl from Birmingham one of the most influential women in the world: "Why would I worry about something like that? The fact of the matter is I've been black all my life. Nobody needs to tell me how to be black."

The Reverend Jesse Jackson leads a protest against the economic policies of President Ronald Reagan in 1985.

bids in the 1980s. Jackson is a longtime civil rights activist and the founder of two social justice organizations, Operation PUSH and the Rainbow Coalition. During his campaigns, he called for an expansion of affirmative action and other social programs to help the poor and disadvantaged. Most political analysts dismissed him as a "fringe candidate" with little chance of winning the nomination. Jackson surprised them by winning 3.5 million votes in the 1984 Democratic primaries and an even more impressive 6.9 million votes in 1988. Those strong showings were not enough to win. However, they were enough to earn Jackson serious consideration as a vice-presidential candidate in 1988. His strength among both black and white voters also gave him a powerful voice in shaping the Democratic Party's presidential platform. At the 1988 Democratic National Convention, Jackson urged delegates to work together to make America a better place. "When we form a great quilt of unity and common ground," he said, "we'll have the power to bring about health care and housing and jobs and education and hope to our Nation."

"A Voice to the Voiceless"

When veterans of the civil rights movement turned from protest to politics in the late 1960s, they hoped to use the power of the black vote to address the many unresolved issues affecting the black community. In some ways they have succeeded. African-American politicians have worked hard to deliver paved streets, running water, and decent housing in black neighborhoods. They have championed programs to improve wages, working conditions, job training, education, health care, and justice for disadvantaged Americans of all races. Congressman Elijah E. Cummings, former chair of the Congressional Black Caucus, sums up the mission of the nation's black political leaders as giving "a voice to the voiceless. We will continue to fight for the millions of Americans who have been excluded or 'neglected' by this nation and its . . . political leadership."

The election of African-American politicians has also led to some disappointments. Like their white counterparts, black political leaders have sometimes proven corrupt or incompetent. More often, dedicated and talented black politicians have faced a long uphill battle against conservative federal policies, economic declines, and widespread social and economic inequality.

Today leaders of the black community believe that one of the most important steps toward solving the many challenges facing black America is increasing black political involvement. In 2000, Representative Jesse L. Jackson Jr. of Illinois, son of the Reverend Jesse Jackson, pointed out that Bill Clinton was

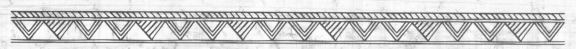

BARACK OBAMA: "WE ARE ONE PEOPLE"

On March 4, 2007, two prominent Democrats marched side by side across the Edmund Pettus Bridge in Selma, Alabama. The politicians were taking part in ceremonies honoring the 1965 Selma-to-Montgomery march.* One was New York's Senator Hillary Rodham Clinton. The other was Senator Barack Obama of Illinois. Speaking before the march, Obama praised the "giants . . . who battled on behalf not just of African-Americans but on behalf of all Americans, who battled for America's soul." The efforts of those civil rights protesters led to the passage of the 1965 Voting Rights Act. And it was that law that gave Obama a serious chance of becoming America's first black president.

Barack Obama visits a Washington, D.C., school during his presidential campaign in 2007.

Barack Obama was born in Honolulu, Hawaii, in 1961. His mother was a white student from Kansas, his father an immigrant from Kenya. Obama later recalled a race-blind childhood in which the fact that "my father . . . was black as pitch, my mother white as milk, barely registered in my mind."

After graduating from Columbia University, Obama earned his law degree at Harvard Law School. In 1996 he was elected to the Illinois State Senate. Eight years later, he became a U.S. senator from Illinois. During his campaign, he gained national fame for his keynote address at the 2004 Democratic National Convention. That rousing speech brought delegates to their feet, cheering as Obama declared, "There is not a liberal America and a conservative America. . . . There is not a black America and a white America and Latino America and Asian America; there's the United States of America. . . . We are one people."

In February 2007 Obama announced his candidacy for president of the United States. As this book goes to press, polls show him running a close second to his chief rival, Senator Clinton. Supporters have embraced Obama's promise of "a more hopeful America." Many also have applauded what he calls his "eat-your-spinach approach." "There's got to be some element of truth telling in this year's campaign," Obama maintains, "because the problems we face are too tough to try to finesse [evade]. If we do that, then we may win an election, but we won't solve the problems."

*For more on the Selma-to-Montgomery march, see volume 9 in this series, *The Civil Rights Movement.*

"elected in 1992 and 1996 with 43 and 47 million votes respectively." At the time Jackson spoke, there were

> 23 million [African Americans] eligible by age and citizenship to vote. The problem is, only about 15 million of us are registered and just 11.5 million actually voted in these two presidential years. . . . That means we are using only half (or less) of our potential political power. . . . There is no other single act than full political participation—registering, voting, educating, and involving ourselves in the public policy debates and issues that confront us every day—that would make as much difference in our material lives as politics.

Eighteen-year-old Shennell Barnes of Newark urges young people to get out and vote at the 2005 New Jersey Hip-Hop Summit.

Hip-hop entrepreneur Russell Simmons puts it more simply: "The most American thing you can do is vote. . . . It empowers you." Simmons is chair of the Hip-Hop Summit Action Network, a nonprofit group that sponsors concertlike events in which prominent rappers encourage members of the audience to register to vote. "Young people are apathetic for the most part," says Simmons, "and many feel locked out of the process. When you vote, you feel like you're part of the process."

Chapter 4

THAT'S BLACK ENTERTAINMENT!

In the past half century, more African Americans than ever before have made their mark in films, television, music, art, literature, and sports. Black entertainers and athletes have often had to struggle against racist attitudes and practices that limited their opportunities in fields dominated by whites. They have achieved their goals through a combination of talent, hard work, and unrelenting determination. In the process they have toppled color barriers, blasted racial stereotypes, and made tremendous contributions to American history and culture.

BIG SCREEN, SMALL SCREEN

At the 74th annual Academy Awards ceremony in 2002, two African Americans received top honors. Denzel Washington was awarded the Oscar for Best Actor. Halle Berry won the Oscar for Best Actress. "Some hailed the Washington-Berry victories as

Opposite: Denzel Washington and Halle Berry won Oscars for Best Actor (for *Training Day*) and Best Actress (for *Monster's Ball*) in 2002.

Sidney Poitier (*right*) and Tony Curtis costarred as escaped convicts in the 1958 action film *The Defiant Ones.*

the beginning of a new era," wrote film critic Roger Ebert, "but it was more clearly the end of an old one: Hollywood's long history of indifference to black talent is clearly over."

The civil rights advances of the 1950s and 1960s brought an end to a long era in which African Americans were limited to minor, stereotyped film roles. Talented black actors and actresses began to appear in major films that showed them relating to white characters in realistic, dignified ways. The first black movie stars also began to emerge. Among them were actors James Earl Jones and Sidney Poitier. Poitier, a multitalented star of stage and screen, was the first black actor to appear as a leading man in Hollywood films. He was the first to be nominated for an Academy Award for Best Actor (for *The Defiant Ones* in 1958) and to win the Best Actor Oscar (for *Lilies of the Field* in 1963). At the 2002 Academy Awards, Poitier was honored with a Lifetime Achievement Award "in recognition of his remarkable accomplishments as an artist and as a human being."

Today a host of African Americans are active in many different areas of the film business. The long list of celebrated black actors and actresses includes Angela Bassett, Don Cheadle, Laurence Fishburne, Jamie Foxx, Morgan Freeman, Danny Glover, Whoopi Goldberg, Cuba Gooding Jr., Louis Gossett Jr., Samuel L. Jackson, Queen Latifah, Martin Lawrence, Eddie Murphy, Jada Pinkett-Smith, Chris Rock, Will Smith, Wesley Snipes, Chris Tucker, and Forest

Director Spike Lee stands outside a New York City theater where his Academy Award–nominated documentary *4 Little Girls* is playing.

Whitaker. Black directors and producers have also brought fresh insights to Hollywood, creating films that speak from the black experience. One of Hollywood's most important and influential directors is Spike Lee. Many of Lee's films explore issues such as racial conflicts and urban violence. His *4 Little Girls*, a movie about the 1963 bombing of Birmingham's Sixteenth Street Baptist Church, was nominated for an Academy Award for Best Feature Documentary in 1997.

African Americans have made their mark in television, too. One of the trailblazers in this field was comedian and actor Bill Cosby. Cosby was the first black actor to star in a weekly TV series, *I Spy*. He later produced and starred in *The Cosby Show*, a popular sitcom portraying an upper-middle-class African-American family.

While African Americans have made great strides in TV and films, the entertainment industry is far from color-blind. Opportunities are still limited for black actresses, especially those who do not meet Hollywood's standard of light-skinned beauty. There are still few African Americans working in behind-the-scene roles, such as camera operators and editors. Most significantly, there are no black studio executives with the power to decide what kinds of movies get made. Scholar and literary critic Henry Louis Gates Jr. believes that it is only a matter of time before American films feature performers chosen for their talent, not the color of their skin. "The growing number of smart, sophisticated black actors and directors is bringing this day much closer," writes Gates. "Scene by scene, film by film, they are changing the industry from the inside. . . . But even they would admit that we still have a very long way to go."

Maya Angelou wrote about growing up in the Jim Crow South in her 1969 autobiography *I Know Why the Caged Bird Sings.*

WORDS AND IMAGES

In 1993 Maya Angelou read her poem "On the Pulse of Morning" at the first inauguration of President Bill Clinton. Her powerful verses asked Americans to

> *Lift up your faces, you have a piercing need*
> *For this bright morning dawning for you.*
> *History, despite its wrenching pain*
> *Cannot be unlived, but if faced*
> *With courage, need not be lived again.*

Maya Angelou, Toni Morrison, Alice Walker, and other modern-day African-American writers have drawn on their life experiences to create compelling works that have received international acclaim. Angelou was raised in rural Arkansas in the days of Jim Crow. During the 1960s, she was active in the civil rights movement. She has written about her childhood and her struggles for racial equality in inspirational poems, essays, and screenplays. Her best-selling autobiography *I Know Why the Caged Bird Sings* describes her journey from abuse and powerlessness to self-worth and dignity.

Toni Morrison insists on being called not a novelist but a "black woman novelist." Her emotionally gripping books deal with African-American characters and communities, especially black women and their children. Morrison's novels include *Sula, Song of Solomon,* and the Pulitzer Prize–winning *Beloved.* In 1993 she became the first African American to receive the Nobel Prize for Literature.

Alice Walker was the youngest of eight children born to poor sharecroppers in rural Georgia. Her novels, poems, short stories, and essays portray the struggles of black women against the "twin afflictions" of racism and sexism. Walker's most famous novel, *The Color Purple*, tells the story of a poor southern woman who triumphs over oppression through positive relationships with other women. *The Color Purple* won the Pulitzer Prize in 1983 and was later adapted into an Oscar-nominated film.

Some African-American artists have worked in paint and stone rather than words. In the 1960s and 1970s, Romare Bearden created powerful paintings and collages reflecting the black experience. In the 1980s Jean-Michel Basquiat captured black city life and the emerging hip-hop culture in dynamic graffiti art. Martin Puryear creates abstract sculptures from wood, stone, and metals. Although he acknowledges the continuing impact of racism in American society, Puryear has never viewed that as an obstacle to his own progress. "Right from the start," he explains, "I thought, No one can keep me from being an artist."

Sunday after Sermon (1969) by the acclaimed African-American artist Romare Bearden

MUSIC AND DANCE

Almost all American popular music has its roots in African-American culture. Rock and roll emerged from black music styles including jazz, gospel, the blues, and R & B (rhythm and blues).* Soul music combined R & B and gospel music. In the 1960s America danced to the Motown sound, a style of recorded soul music with a thumping backbeat. In the late 1970s, rap music got its start among black DJs in the Bronx neighborhoods of New York City.

The list of talented black musical performers and composers is nearly endless. Dynamic singer-songwriter James Brown was revered as the "Godfather of Soul." Marvin Gaye, Stevie Wonder, and vocal groups the Temptations, the Four Tops, and Diana Ross and the Supremes topped the list of Motown's best-selling recording artists. Chuck Berry, Ray Charles, Aretha Franklin, and Jimi Hendrix are among the many black musical

*For more on jazz and the blues, see volume 7 in this series, *The Harlem Renaissance.*

talents inducted into the Rock and Roll Hall of Fame. Trumpeters Miles Davis and Wynton Marsalis have been called two of the most influential jazz musicians of the twentieth century. In the world of rap and hip-hop, some of today's hottest artists include 50 Cent (Curtis Jackson), Snoop Dogg (Cordozar Broadus), Ice Cube (O'Shea Jackson), Ludacris (Christopher Bridges), and Jay-Z (Shawn Carter).

African Americans have also made their mark in the worlds of classical music and dance. Leontyne Price and Jessye Norman are two of America's most admired opera singers. Arthur Mitchell was the first black principal dancer of a major American ballet company. He also founded the country's first black classical ballet company, the Dance Theatre of Harlem. Alvin Ailey created the internationally acclaimed American Dance Theater. Ailey employed dancers of different races and body types in his company, because he "wanted to celebrate the differences in people." The many black dancers who flourished under his guidance included tall, elegant Judith Jamison, current director of the Alvin Ailey American Dance Theater.

James Brown thrilled audiences with his soulful songs and high-energy performing style.

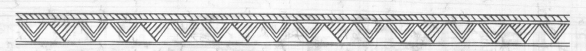

BEYONCÉ KNOWLES:
"I LIKE TO CHALLENGE MYSELF"

When Beyoncé Knowles was nine years old, she formed an R & B singing group with her cousin and two friends. The four girls rehearsed in their backyards. They tried out their musical numbers on the customers in Beyoncé's mother's beauty shop. Their first break came with a 1992 appearance on television's *Star Search*. The foursome did not win the competition. However, Beyoncé's father, Matthew Knowles, was so impressed by their talent and drive that he quit his job to help his daughter and her friends pursue their dream of a professional singing career.

Singer, songwriter, actress, and clothing designer Beyoncé Knowles

Beyoncé's group, Destiny's Child, released their first single in 1997. "No, No, No" soared to the top of the pop charts. The group followed that success with several other hit songs and award-winning albums. In 2003 Beyoncé launched her solo career with the album *Dangerously in Love*. The multimillion-selling disk earned five Grammy awards, confirming her status as one of R & B's premier singers, songwriters, and producers. The talented young star has also branched out into acting, with acclaimed roles in films including *Dreamgirls* and *The Fighting Temptations*.

Throughout her rise to fame, Beyoncé has remained true to her roots. She and her mother, Tina, have started their own successful clothing line, House of Dereon, which they named after Tina's mother. Beyoncé's father, Matthew, remains a hands-on manager who measures his daughter's success not "on the number of records she sells" but instead "on how proud I am that she is a genuine good person. . . . That she is respectful and honest. That she gives back to her community and that she has so much love for her family."

For Beyoncé herself, success has been "more beautiful than you could ever imagine but it's also harder than you ever imagined. Like everything in life, there are sacrifices . . . but it's worth it." This confident, hardworking young woman has a restless spirit that constantly pushes her to raise the bar. "Everything that I do creatively has to make me work harder, and hopefully steer me in a direction I've never gone before," she says. "I like to challenge myself and all those around me to get the very best creatively."

Revolutionizing Sports

It has been about sixty years since Jackie Robinson broke the color barrier in professional baseball. Today it is hard to imagine what the sports world would be like without the contributions of African-American athletes. In nearly every major sport, black athletes have raised the level of competition, often bringing a daring, creative new style that has changed the way the games are played. "When Whites controlled many of the sports," observed tennis champion Arthur Ashe, "there was not enough spontaneity, not enough creativity, not enough innovation, not enough willingness to try different things to see if they would work. Blacks have certainly brought those elements to the arenas, diamonds and courts."

Nowhere is the impact of black athletes more obvious than in basketball. When basketball was a whites-only sport, it was much slower and more predictable. Wilt Chamberlain, Bill Russell, Connie Hawkins, Elgin Baylor, Kareem Abdul-Jabbar, and other African-American players introduced a faster, more physical, more freewheeling style of play. In the 1980s Michael Jordan became an American hero with his combination of speed, grace, power, and inventiveness. Today a new generation of black players, including Lebron James, Dwyane Wade, and Gilbert Arenas, dominate the NBA. These young players grew up admiring Jordan not only for his skills on the court but also for his image as one of the world's most successful and respected black businessmen.

Alvin Ailey (*center*), performing with members of his world-famous American Dance Theater in 1965

Michael Jordan's high-flying heroics on the basketball court earned him the nickname Air Jordan.

Black athletes have also raised the bar in other team sports. Hank Aaron became Major League Baseball's home-run king in 1974 when he broke the "unbreakable" record held by the legendary Babe Ruth. In 2007 Barry Bonds passed Aaron's career record of 755 home runs. (Bonds's achievement was overshadowed by controversy over his alleged use of performance-enhancing drugs.) In football Emmitt Smith leads all running backs with 166 career touchdowns and holds the NFL record for rushing yards. Previous rushing records were set by black football greats Walter Payton and Jim Brown. Linebacker Lawrence Taylor is a three-time NFL Defensive Player of the Year who has played in ten Pro Bowls.

Florence Griffith Joyner brought both speed and style to track and field. At the 1988 Olympics, "Flo Jo" won three gold medals and set world records in the 100- and 200-meter sprints. She also captured the world's attention with her one-legged running outfits and brightly painted fingernails.

Other black athletes who revolutionized their sports have included tennis greats Althea Gibson and Arthur Ashe.

Gibson was the first African American to win the prestigious Wimbledon title. Ashe was the first black man to win Wimbledon, along with many of the world's other major tennis tournaments.

Tiger Woods is golf's first black superstar.* As of 2007, he had won twelve major championships and fifty-seven tournaments worldwide. While Tiger is a fierce competitor with "a love and a passion for getting that ball in the hole," he has recently found something that gives him even greater satisfaction. In 2006 he opened the first Tiger Woods Learning Center in Southern California. The $25 million facility offers children from different backgrounds state-of-the-art programs to help them prepare for college and careers. "Golf is what I do," says Tiger. "It's definitely not who I am. . . . I don't get the satisfaction [from golf] that I get from building this and helping kids and putting a smile on their face and giving them hope."

Track-and-field champion Florence Griffith Joyner in action at the 1988 Summer Olympics in Seoul, South Korea

*Tiger, who has a mixed racial heritage, calls himself "Cablinasian," a made-up term that stands for "Caucasian-black-Indian-Asian."

DWYANE WADE:
"I'VE ONLY SCRATCHED THE SURFACE"

For Dwyane Wade, success was no sure thing. Born in 1982, Dwyane spent his early years in the tough South Side neighborhood of Chicago. His single mom struggled to make ends meet. At age eight he was sent to live with his father in a Chicago suburb that he describes as "rough [but] a big step up. You could be outside late at night and not hear gunshots."

In high school Dwyane was an exceptional basketball player, but his grades were not good enough for any of the major college programs to recruit him. He decided

Above: Dwyane Wade shows off his trophies after leading the Miami Heat to victory over the Dallas Mavericks in the 2006 NBA Finals.

to continue his education at Marquette University in Milwaukee, Wisconsin. He spent his freshman year working to improve in both academics and basketball. When he finally got to play for the Marquette Golden Eagles, he led the team to two Final Four play-offs. After his electrifying performance in the 2003 finals, he was ranked among the top college players in the nation. The following year he entered the NBA draft. The Miami Heat took him in the first round.

In Miami, Dwyane quickly established himself as one of the sport's leading guards. He scored more postseason points in his first three seasons than any other player in NBA history. In 2006 he led the Heat to their first NBA championship. He also earned honors including the NBA Finals Most Valuable Player award and the *Sports Illustrated* Sportsman of the Year.

Fellow players and coaches have praised Dwyane not only for his amazing playing skills but also for his unselfish conduct both on and off the court. "In this day and age, so many people flash their agenda," says Tom Crean, his former coach at Marquette. "His agenda is about winning, being a good teammate, being a good husband and a good father." When Dwyane has a bad game, he still calls his college and high school coaches for advice. He still spends hours each summer at his old high school gym, shooting baskets and signing jerseys for local students. He is devoted to his wife, Siohvaughn, and their two children, Zaire and Zion. He recently founded the Dwyane Wade Foundation to "give back a little of what I have received." The nonprofit foundation supports programs to help underprivileged young people reach their educational and athletic goals.

Today Dwyane Wade is living the life he always dreamed of, but he is still working hard to improve his game. "I've only scratched the surface of where I want to be in my career," he maintains. "I'm going to continue to get better and do what I can to help my team be the best it can possibly be."

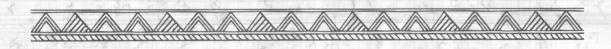

Chapter 5

SOCIAL JUSTICE

In 2006 Harold Ford Jr. ran as the Democratic candidate for the Senate in Tennessee. The race was one of the most hotly contested battles of the midterm elections. The Democrats needed to win just six seats nationwide to wrest control of the Senate from the Republicans. Determined to hold on to Tennessee, the Republican National Committee (RNC) poured support into the campaign of Ford's opponent, white businessman Bob Corker. Two weeks before the election, polls showed the candidates running neck and neck. Harold Ford had a good chance of becoming the first black senator elected in the South since Reconstruction.

Then the RNC ran a commercial. The ad featured a series of people talking sarcastically about Ford. One was a bare-shouldered white actress who declared, "I met Harold at the Playboy party." With a wink at the camera, the woman whispered, "Harold, call me."

Opposite: Heavyweight boxing champion Evander Holyfield shows his support for the family of James Byrd Jr., who was murdered by white racists in Texas in 1998.

Critics denounced the campaign ad, calling it an attempt to appeal to old-style racist fears by linking the young black candidate with an attractive white woman. After several days the RNC stopped running the ad. Two weeks later, Bob Corker won the election by a narrow margin. It is impossible to say how great a role race played in Ford's defeat. But the controversy made at least one point clear: racism remains a very real and divisive issue in American society.

THE RACIAL DIVIDE

In a 1999 survey, African Americans were more than twice as likely as whites to say that blacks were "discriminated against in this society a lot." A 2006 poll found that 53 percent of whites thought that racial minorities had equal job opportunities, compared to only 17 percent of blacks. Many analysts believe that these conflicting views on racism are the result of different life experiences. White Americans enjoy the privileges that come with whiteness in a racist society, often without even being aware of it. They do not experience the kinds of racial prejudice that blacks encounter all the time.

Racism can show itself in subtle ways. "Every day that you live as a black person," explained one college student, "you're reminded how you're perceived in society. You walk the streets at night; white people cross the streets . . . to not be on the same side. . . . White men tighten their grip on their women. I've seen people turn around [as if] they're going to take blows from me." Donna Pearson, a light-skinned black woman who lived in an upper-middle-class New Jersey neighborhood, found that "racism still exists, but it's more quiet. It's kept behind closed doors. . . . People sometimes think I'm white, and they'll say

In 2005 former Ku Klux Klan leader Edgar Ray Killen was convicted of organizing the 1964 murders of three civil rights workers in Mississippi.

things and I'll say, excuse me, I'm African American too. And all of a sudden their face gets red."

Nearly one out of every four African Americans seeking to rent an apartment or buy a home experiences racial discrimination. Racism also can result in discrimination in traditionally white public accommodations. A health club or country club may discourage African Americans from joining for fear of "scaring away" white customers. A restaurant may seat white customers while blacks stand and wait. In the 1990s restaurant chains including Denny's, Shoney's, and the International House of Pancakes faced lawsuits for discriminating against black customers. At a Denny's in San Jose, California, a group of black teenagers were refused service unless they paid in advance. In Annapolis, Maryland, six African-American Secret Service agents sued the chain after they waited an hour for their food while white patrons were promptly served. Denny's paid millions of dollars to settle all the lawsuits. The company also agreed to develop a program to ensure that its employees treat all customers fairly.

In extreme cases racism can lead to violent hate crimes. In 1998 a black man named James Byrd Jr. was tortured and killed by three young white men in Jasper, Texas. In 1989 sixteen-year-old Yusef Hawkins of Brooklyn, New York, was beaten and shot to death by a gang of white teenagers who had mistaken him for another black youth. "Yusef lost his life because he was black and walking through a white neighborhood," wrote Molefi Kete Asante, professor of African-American studies at Temple University. Asante compares daily life for a black American to walking down a road filled with "potholes of racial hostility. . . . You are minding your own business, with

Two men mourn outside the Brooklyn church where funeral services are being held for sixteen-year-old hate crime victim Yusef Hawkins.

whites far away from your mind, until you read the newspaper, watch a television program, hear a radio commentator, or run into someone on the job whose only purpose that day is to . . . 'put Africans in their place.'"

RACISM IN LAW ENFORCEMENT

In 1991 a black motorist named Rodney King led police in Los Angeles, California, on a high-speed chase. When King was finally stopped, four white officers punched, kicked, and clubbed him. He suffered a fractured skull, a shattered eye socket, and other serious injuries. An onlooker captured the entire incident on videotape. Many viewers who watched the beating on TV were convinced that the police had used excessive force. In April 1992 a nearly all-white jury disagreed, clearing the officers of all charges. That verdict sparked a four-day riot in Los Angeles, which killed fifty-five people and left more than two thousand injured. (In a later federal trial, a more racially diverse jury found two of the officers guilty of violating King's civil rights.)

Many social analysts have pointed to incidents such as the Rodney King case as evidence of racism by the police against blacks. Studies of law enforcement have added weight to their claims. One analysis of police searches in Maryland, for example, showed that about 75 percent of the motorists driving over the speed limit on an interstate highway were white, while about 17 percent were black. Meanwhile, out of all the drivers stopped and searched by the Maryland State Police, about 80 percent were black.

The reason behind those lopsided numbers was "racial profiling." Racial profiling is any police action in which a person is

A member of the Guardian Angels, a citizens patrol group, calls for racial harmony during the trial of four Los Angeles police officers charged in the 1991 beating death of black motorist Rodney King.

treated as a suspect because of his or her race or nationality. Police officers engaging in racial profiling may pull over black drivers for minor traffic violations, while overlooking the same violations by whites. African Americans who drive expensive cars or travel through white neighborhoods may be stopped by police who assume that they stole their cars or are planning a crime. Blacks are far more likely than whites to be stopped and questioned when walking on city sidewalks. They are also more likely to be tailed by security guards in malls and searched by airport security personnel.

Racial profiling is inconvenient and humiliating. It can also be lethal. "There's a perception that black male youth are more dangerous, more violent and more likely to be armed than their white counterparts," says New York lawyer Ron Kuby. "That concern about young black men permeates the police depart-

Harlem artist Hulbert Waldroup works on a mural of Amadou Diallo, a West African immigrant gunned down by New York City police outside his home in 1999.

ment and results in police shooting black youth under circumstances where they would not shoot white people."

The inequalities in the treatment of blacks and whites continue after suspects are arrested for crimes. For example, one federal study found that African Americans made up 35 percent of all those arrested for drug possession but 74 percent of those sentenced to prison for the crime.

Inequalities in law enforcement have contributed to a prison system in which African Americans, who compose about 13 percent of the total U.S. population, account for about half of all those in prison or jail. In 2005 about 12 percent of all black males aged twenty-five to twenty-nine were imprisoned, compared to less than 2 percent of white males in the same age group. That translates into thousands of young black mothers struggling to support their families on their own and thousands of black children growing up without fathers. The toll on black families and communities is beyond measure. *Chicago Tribune* columnist Salim Muwakkil has called it a "social emergency" that has generated "little public awareness. . . . In this country, we've learned to link complexion to crime."

THE HEALTH CARE CRISIS

Today a majority of African-American children are living in single-parent households or being raised by someone other than a parent. Many of these children will grow up in inner-city communities, amid run-down housing, unsafe streets, high unemployment, and failing schools. "It's hard to grow up in that kind of environment," observed twenty-one-year-old Domonique Williams of Philadelphia, "and do the right thing when everything around you isn't right."

One of the most deadly challenges facing young African Americans is an explosive health crisis. Poverty, inadequate health care and health insurance, substandard living conditions, and other factors have resulted in a shorter life expectancy for black Americans than for whites. Blacks have higher rates of obesity, diabetes, high blood pressure, heart disease, and some types of cancers. While the pregnancy rate among young black girls has declined in recent decades, they are still almost twice as likely as white girls to become parents too soon.

The number-one health threat to the black community is the AIDS epidemic. Hundreds of thousands of African Americans across the nation have contracted the HIV virus that causes AIDS. In 2005 black Americans accounted for about half of all new HIV cases. One recent study found that young

A traveling educator visits a classroom in South Carolina to teach children about health.

black women are seven times more likely than young white women to be infected with HIV.

Solving all these life-and-death problems will require a multipronged approach that includes improved access to low-cost medical care and better health education. Brenda Dalton, director of student health services at Spelman College in Atlanta, believes that the key is reaching out to young people and their parents. "Folks have got to know what is available," says Dalton. "Take it to the grocery store or the neighborhood car wash. Sometimes you have to pack it up and take it on the road. If you impact one person, it's like fire, it spreads." Carol Matthews, co-director of the Harlem Adolescent Pregnancy Prevention Initiative, agrees. The Harlem initiative uses teenagers to teach other teens. Youngsters take part in programs including self-esteem seminars and job fairs. "It's not just about teaching kids how to say no to sex," says Matthews, "but how to say yes to a more healthy lifestyle and bright future."

TAVIS SMILEY:
"WE ARE THE MASTERS OF
OUR DESTINY"

Tavis Smiley likes to tell the story of the gazelle and the lion. When the gazelle wakes up in the morning, it knows that there is something out there ready to eat it. When the lion wakes up, it knows that it must eat or starve. "The point is," says Smiley, "it doesn't matter if you're a gazelle or a lion, you'd better wake up in the morning running."

Tavis Smiley has been running—and encouraging black America to keep up—for nearly twenty years. As a young man deeply concerned about the many problems facing the black community, he set out to make a positive impact through education and empowerment. In 1991 he started the *Smiley Report*, a daily radio news commentary. Next came the popular Black Entertainment Television talk show *BET Tonight with Tavis Smiley*, which featured interviews with personalities ranging from Bill Clinton to Pope John Paul II to Ice Cube.

Author, journalist, and talk show host Tavis Smiley

The energetic journalist-activist has also hosted a weekly program on National Public Radio and a late-night talk show on PBS. He has written several books, including *Doing What's Right, Never Mind Success . . . Go for Greatness,* and *How to Make Black America Better.* His *Covenant with Black America* was the first book published by a black publishing company to hit number one on the *New York Times* best-seller list. Smiley credits the book's success to the fact that "black folk are thirsty for information about the state of Black America and for an action agenda they can use to address the issues that impact our communities."

The Covenant with Black America is a collection of essays by leading black scholars and activists on issues ranging from health and education to the criminal justice system and economic empowerment. It offers practical suggestions on steps that black individuals and communities can take to address their political, economic, and social concerns. African Americans across the nation have responded enthusiastically to the book's call to action. Through efforts such as health workshops, academic and cultural programs, and recovery projects in flood-ravaged New Orleans, they have improved their own lives and the lives of others in their families and communities.

Tavis Smiley's current mission is to build on "the energy generated by *The Covenant* and . . . move it to *sustained, coordinated, long-term* action. We are the masters of our destiny. We can be the catalysts for dramatic change in our own lives and in the life of our community, daring to believe that we have the power and the ability to change the course of history. . . . When we make Black America better, we make *all* of America better."

AFTER THE FLOODS

In August 2005 Hurricane Katrina slammed the Gulf Coast. The high winds caused a devastating surge of water from the Gulf of Mexico into New Orleans. That storm surge overwhelmed the system of floodwalls, or levees, built to hold back the Mississippi River and Lake Pontchartrain. Rising floodwaters trapped tens of thousands of people who had been unable to evacuate before the storm. Many crowded into makeshift shelters, including the Louisiana Superdome. Conditions there quickly went from bad to worse, with backed-up toilets, no air conditioning, and no food or water. Americans watching the horrifying images on TV could not help but notice one disquieting fact: the overwhelming majority of desperate refugees in New Orleans were black.

Before Hurricane Katrina, 84 percent of the people living in poverty in New Orleans were African Americans. Most poor blacks lived in the city's low-lying neighborhoods, which bore the brunt of the flooding. More than two years later, those neighborhoods remain largely deserted. Black homeowners are still struggling to find the money to rebuild, while housing projects once occupied mainly by poor blacks are boarded up and surrounded by chain-link fences.

Despite all their losses, the black residents of New Orleans cling to hope. In a recent survey, 67 percent of blacks were convinced that the devastated city would return to normal, compared to 52 percent of whites. "If you wonder how optimism can flourish the most among those who have the least," wrote columnist Leonard Pitts Jr., "well, maybe when you've been weaned on hardship, hardship doesn't impress you. You do what you've got to do, suffer what you've got to suffer, to get where you've got to get."

The final chapters in the story of New Orleans and the broader history of black America have not been written yet. The pages to come will be written by people like you, the reader. We live in an age of both hope and despair. Great progress has been made in the four-hundred-year black freedom struggle. Great challenges remain. It will take the combined energies of Americans of all races to complete the journey toward a true democracy in which every citizen has a fair chance to reach his or her full potential. It will take people like Lisa Rollins, an African-American girl from Philadelphia who urges us to "step up and take the lead for our own problems. Nowadays, you see a lot of people saying, 'I can't be this, I can't do this.' . . . If you step back and take a look at yourself, you can do whatever you want to do."

Desperate residents plead for rescue from a New Orleans rooftop in the aftermath of Hurricane Katrina.

Glossary

affirmative action A policy in which members of minority groups (or women) are given special preference in order to make up for the effects of past discrimination and improve their educational or employment opportunities.

civil rights movement The nonviolent struggle to end racial discrimination and segregation in the United States; the modern civil rights movement took place in the 1950s and 1960s.

entrepreneur A person who is willing to take risks in business in order to make a profit.

Jim Crow Laws and practices designed to segregate African Americans, stripping them of their political and civil rights; the Jim Crow era began around the end of Reconstruction.

lower South The former slaveholding states of the South.

lynch To lawlessly execute a person by mob action, often by hanging.

quota A fixed number or percentage of people, such as minority group members or women, who must be admitted to a school or hired by a business under affirmative action guidelines.

racial diversity The presence of people from different races and backgrounds in schools or the workplace.

Reconstruction The period from 1865 to 1877, during which the former Confederate states were placed under military rule before being readmitted to the Union.

segregation The practice of separating one race from another by setting up separate housing, schools, and other public facilities.

stereotypes Exaggerated, usually negative images of people belonging to a particular ethnic group, region, or religion.

transatlantic slave trade The capture of men, women, and children in Africa and the transporting of those captives into slavery in the Americas.

To Find Out More

BOOKS

Marzilli, Alan. *Affirmative Action.* Philadelphia: Chelsea House, 2004.

Thomas, Velma Maia. *We Shall Not Be Moved: The Passage from the Great Migration to the Million Man March.* New York: Crown, 2002.

Treanor, Nick, ed. *The Civil Rights Movement.* San Diego, CA: Greenhaven Press, 2003.

Williams, Mary E. *Issues in Racism.* San Diego, CA: Lucent Books, 2000.

FACING THE FUTURE

Young, Mitchell, ed. *Racial Discrimination.* Farmington Hills, MI: Greenhaven Press, 2006.

WEB SITES

African American World for Kids. PBS Kids.
   http://pbskids.org/aaworld
Biography: Celebrating Our Black History. A&E Television Networks.
   http://www.biography.com/blackhistory
The eZine. Multiple Shades of You Online.
   http://www.msoyonline.com/theezine/index.htm
The Million Man March. © 1996 The Afro-American Newspaper Company of Baltimore, Inc.
   http://www.afro.com/history/million/millman.html
The Millions More Movement. © 2007 Million Man March.
   http://www.millionsmoremovement.com/index_flash.html
Trailblazers for the Next Generation: Contemporary African-American History Makers. Sonya Stinson. The Black Collegian Online.
   http://www.black-collegian.com/african/trailblzr.shtml

Selected Bibliography

Asante, Molefi Kete. *Erasing Racism: The Survival of the American Nation.* Amherst, NY: Prometheus Books, 2003.

Fairclough, Adam. *Better Day Coming: Blacks and Equality, 1890–2000.* New York: Viking, 2001.

Feagin, Joe R., and Melvin P. Sikes. *Living with Racism: The Black Middle-Class Experience.* Boston: Beacon Press, 1994.

Gates, Henry Louis, Jr. *America Behind the Color Line: Dialogues with African Americans.* New York: Warner Books, 2004.

Gates, Henry Louis, Jr., and Cornel West. *The African American Century: How Black Americans Have Shaped Our Country.* New York: Free Press, 2000.

Graves, Earl G. *How to Succeed in Business Without Being White.* New York: HarperCollins, 1997.

Lagerloef, Janet. "The Pied Piper of Healing." *Hope* magazine, Winter 2001.

Loury, Glenn C. *The Anatomy of Racial Inequality.* Cambridge, MA: Harvard University Press, 2001.

Ogletree, Charles J., Jr. *All Deliberate Speed: Reflections on the First Half Century of Brown v. Board of Education.* New York: W. W. Norton, 2004.

Oliver, Melvin L., and Thomas M. Shapiro. *Black Wealth/White Wealth.* New

York: Routledge, 1995.

Orfield, Gary, Daniel Losen, Johanna Wald, and Christopher B. Swanson. *Losing Our Future: How Minority Youth Are Being Left Behind by the Graduation Rate Crisis.* A Joint Release by The Civil Rights Project at Harvard University, The Urban Institute, Advocates for Children of New York, and The Civil Society Institute.
http://www.urban.org/publications/410936.html

Rubel, David. *The Coming Free: The Struggle for African-American Equality.* New York: DK Publishing, 2005.

Smiley, Tavis. *The Covenant in Action.* Carlsbad, CA: Smiley Books, 2006.

———, ed. *How to Make Black America Better.* New York: Doubleday, 2001.

Wallis, Claudia, and Sonja Steptoe. "Report Card on No Child Left Behind." *Time,* June 4, 2007.

Notes on Quotes

Introduction

p. 9, "unity, atonement, and brotherhood": "Million Man March" at
http://photo2.si.edu/mmm/mmm.html

p. 9, "the sense that": Anyi Howell, "NPR Youth Radio: Mixed Signals from Millions More," at
http://www.npr.org/templates/story/story.php?stryId=4961463

p. 9, "If there is no struggle": Frederick Douglass, "No Struggle, No Progress," at http://academic.udayton.edu/race/poetry/nostruggle.htm

p. 9, "We have known": "The Continuing Struggle: Howard L. Fuller, Speech before the BAEO Symposium, March 2, 2001," at
http://www.heartland.org/Article.cfm?artId=9933

Chapter 1: The Crisis in Education

p. 11, "What happened here": "One America for Today, Tomorrow and Forever, Clinton Says," *Arkansas Online,* at
http://www.ardemgaz.com/prev/central/prestext26.html

p. 12, "I think each of us": "Little Rock 9 Recognized for Heroism" at
http://www.ardemgaz.com/prev/central/abxnine10.html

p. 12, "opportunity to change": "Little Rock Nine Awarded Congressional Gold Medals" at
http://www.cnn.com/US/9911/09/little.rock.nine.02/index.html#1

p. 14, "We seek not just": "Lyndon B. Johnson, 'To Fulfill These Rights': Commencement Address at Howard University, June 4, 1965," at

http://score.rims.k12.ca.us/activity/lbj/lbjspeech.html

p. 20, "We must give": "The Continuing Struggle: Howard L. Fuller, Speech before the BAEO Symposium, March 2, 2001," at http://www.heartland.org/Article.cfm?artId=9933

p. 21, "change lives and mend": Gates, *America Behind the Color Line*, p. 425.

p. 21, "I want students": "The National Teachers Hall of Fame: Dr. Emiel Hamberlin, 2001 Inductee," at http://www.nthf.org/inductee/hamberlin.htm

p. 21, "He spent countless hours": ibid.

Chapter 2: The Economic Divide

p. 23, "the idea of wanting": "Earl Gilbert Graves, Jr. Biography," *Encyclopedia of World Biography*, at http://www.bookrags.com/biography/earl-gilbert-graves-jr

p. 24, "come together": Earl G. Graves, "Leveraging Our Power," in Smiley, *How to Make Black America Better*, pp. 108, 109.

p. 25, "When it is cold": "The State of Black America: Economics" at www.blackamericaweb.com

p. 27, "The blacks think": "Americans Vent Anger at Affirmative Action," *Washington Post*, March 24, 1995, at http://www.washingtonpost.com/wp-srv/politics/special/affirm/stories/aa032495.htm

pp. 27–28, "a triple-burn for African Americans": Gene Sperling, "Budget Problems: Bush Economics Leave Most African Americans Behind," *The Crisis*, March/April 2004, at http://findarticles.com/p/articles/mi_qa4081/is_200403/ai_n9364163

p. 28, "only eight": Melvin Oliver, "American Dream? How Government Initiatives Made Blacks House Poor," *The Crisis*, September/October 2003, at http://findarticles.com/p/articles/mi_qa4081/is_200309/ai_n9297805

p. 30, "This is a system": Oliver and Shapiro, *Black Wealth/White Wealth*, p. 21.

p. 30, 33, "It is important": Earl G. Graves, "Dreams Imagined . . . Aspirations Achieved: A Letter to My Grandchildren," *Black Enterprise*, August 2000, at http://findarticles.com/p/articles/mi_m1365/is_1_31/ai_63974355

p. 31, "You can get there" and "whatever your goal": "Oprah Winfrey Quotes" at http://womenshistory.about.com/cs/quotes/a/oprah_winfrey.htm

p. 31, "I believe": "The Oprah Winfrey Leadership Academy Foundation" at http://www.oprah.com/ophilanthropy/owlaf/owlaf_landing.jhtml

p. 32, "You have to stick": "Hip-Hopping to the Top: Simmons' Rise to Success" at http://www.evancarmichael.com/Famous-Entrepreneurs/544/HipHopping-to-the-Top-Simmons-Rise-to-Success.html

Chapter 3: Political Power

p. 36, "A profound lesson": Smiley, *The Covenant in Action*, p. 3.

p. 37, "promote the public welfare": "A Voice: African American Voices in Congress" at http://www.avoiceonline.org/cbc/history.html

p. 38, "because someone had to": Shirley Chisholm, *The Good Fight* (New York: Harper & Row, 1973), pp. 3–4.

p. 39, "twice as good" and "I remember more": "Condi: The Girl Who Cracked the Ice," *Sunday Times*, November 21, 2004, at http://timesonline.co.uk/tol/news/article393371.ece

p. 39, "so radically different": Eugene Robinson, "Why Rice Can't See," *Washington Post*, October 25, 2005, p. A21.

p. 39, "Why would I worry": "Interview with Bill O'Reilly of the O'Reilly Factor on Fox News," September 14, 2005, at http://www.state.gov/secretary/rm/2005/53155.htm

pp. 40–41, "When we form": "Address by the Reverend Jesse Louis Jackson, July 19, 1988" at http://www.pbs.org/wgbh/pages/frontline/jesse/speeches/jesse88speech.html

p. 41, "a voice to the voiceless": Elijah E. Cummings, "Honoring Shirley Chisholm's Vision," *The Baltimore Afro-American Newspaper*, January 8, 2005, at http://www.house.gov/cummings/articles/art05_01.htm

pp. 41, 43, "elected in 1992" and "23 million": Smiley, *How to Make Black America Better*, pp. 101, 102.

p. 42, "We are one people": "Barack Obama 2004 Democratic National Convention Keynote Address," July 27, 2004, at http://www.american rhetoric.com/speeches/convention2004/barackobama2004dnc.htm

p. 42, "giants . . . who battled": "Clinton and Obama Unite in Pleas to Blacks," *New York Times*, March 5, 2007.

p. 42, "my father . . . was black": "Barack Obama Biography" at http://www.barackobamabiography.com

p. 42, "There is not": "Barack Obama 2004 Democratic National Convention Keynote Address," July 27, 2004, at http://www.americanrhetoric.com/speeches/convention2004/barackobama2004dnc.htm

p. 42, "a more hopeful America": "Obama Declares White House Candidacy," February 10, 2007, at http://www.newsmax.com/archives/articles/2007/2/10/113431.shtml

p. 42, "eat-your-spinach" and "There's got to be": Karen Tumulty, "The Candor Candidate: Why Obama Tells People What They Don't Want to Hear," *Time*, June 11, 2007, pp. 33, 35.

p. 43, "The most American thing" and "Young people are": "Here & Now: Russell Simmons on Voting," wbur.org, aired November 4, 2003, at http://www.here-now.org/shows/2003/11/20031104_13.asp

Chapter 4: That's Black Entertainment!

pp. 45–46, "Some hailed the Washington-Berry": "African-Americans in Motion Pictures: The Past and the Present" at http://www.liu.edu/cwis/CWP/library/african/movies.htm

p. 46, "in recognition of his remarkable": "2001 Academy Awards Winners and History" at http://www.filmsite.org/aa01.html

p. 48, "The growing number": Gates, *America Behind the Color Line*, p. 230.

p. 48, "Lift up your faces": "Inaugural Poem: Maya Angelou, 20 January 1993" at http://poetry.eserver.org/angelou.html

p. 49, "black woman novelist": "Toni Morrison Biography" at http://www.bookrags.com/biography/toni-morrison-aya/

p. 49, "twin afflictions": "Alice Walker" at http://www.gale.com/free_resources/bhm/bio/walker_a.htm

p. 49, "Right from the start": "Artist: Martin Puryear" at http://www.cnn.com/SPECIALS/2001/americasbest/pro.mpuryear.html

p. 51, "wanted to celebrate": Gates and West, *The African-American Century*, p. 315.

p. 52, "I like to challenge myself": "About Beyoncé" at http://www.beyonceonline.com/main.html

p. 52, "on the number": "Matthew Knowles Responds to Beyoncé B'Day Rumors" at http://top40.about.com/b/a/208371.htm

p. 52, "more beautiful": "Beyoncé Knowles: Beyond Destiny" at http://www.beatboxbetty.com/celebetty/beyonceknowles/beyonceknowles/beyonceknowles.htm

p. 52, "Everything that I do": "About Beyoncé" at http://www.beyonceonline.com/main.html

p. 53, "When Whites controlled": "Redefining the Limits: Contributions and Sports Records of Afro American Athletes," *Ebony*, August 1991, at http://findarticles.com/p/articles/mi_m1077/is_n10_v46/ai_11098742

p. 55, "a love and a passion": "Tiger Woods Up Close and Personal," 60 *Minutes*, September 3, 2006, at http://www.cbsnews.com/stories/2006/03/23/60minutes/main1433767.shtml

p. 55, "Golf is what I do": ibid.

p. 56, "I've only scratched": "Dwyane Wade" at http://www.mcdavidusa.com/endorsements/dwyanewade.asp

p. 56, "rough [but] a big step": "Heat Star Wade-ing into Special Territory,"
USA Today, February 17, 2005, at http://www.usatoday.com/sports/
basketball/nba/heat/2005-02-17-wade-all-star_x.htm

p. 57, "In this day and age": ibid.

p. 57, "give back a little": "The Dwyane Wade Foundation" at
http://www.dwyanewade.com/fans/foundation.php

Chapter 5: Social Justice

p. 59, "I met Harold": "Elections Loom; Now Is the Time for Negative Ads"
at http://www.npr.org/templates/story/story.php?storyId=6383830

p. 60, "discriminated against in this society": "Race and Ethnicity" at
http://www.pollingreport.com/race.htm

p. 60, "Every day that you live": Feagin, *Living with Racism*, p. 72.

p. 60, "racism still exists": Gates, *America Behind the Color Line*, p. 101.

p. 62, "Yusef lost his life": Asante, *Erasing Racism*, p. 232.

p. 62, "potholes of racial hostility": ibid., p. 234.

p. 64, "There's a perception": "Race a Complicated Issue in NYC Shooting,"
December 2, 2006, at http://www.washingtonpost.com/wp-dyn/
content/article/2006/12/02/AR2006120200444.html

p. 66, "social emergency": "The Drug War's Toll on the Black Community" at
http://www.chicagomediawatch.org/02_2_black.shtml

p. 66, "It's hard to grow up": Leonard Pitts Jr., "Stop Blaming Others for Failure," *Times Herald-Record*, June 16, 2007, at http://www.recordonline.com/
apps/pbcs.dii/article?AID=/20070616/OPINION/706160305

p. 67, "Folks have got": Lorinda Bullock, "The Explosive Health Crisis That
No One Talks About," *Ebony*, December 2003, at
http://findarticles.com/p/articles/mi_m1077/is_2_59/ai_110962916/pg_2

p. 67, "It's not just about": ibid.

p. 68, "We are the masters": Smiley, *The Covenant in Action*, p. 90.

p. 68, "The point is": Smiley, *How to Make Black America Better*, p. xiv.

p. 69, "black folk are thirsty": Smiley, *The Covenant in Action*, p. xiii.

p. 69, "the energy generated": ibid., p. 90.

p. 70, "If you wonder": Leonard Pitts Jr., "At Large: Hardest-Hit Victims Are
the Most Optimistic," *Miami Herald*, March 2006, at
http://findarticles.com/p/articles/mi_kmtmh/is_200603/ai_n16096594

p. 71, "step up and take": Leonard Pitts Jr., "Stop Blaming Others for Failure,"
Times Herald-Record, June 16, 2007, at http://www.recordonline.com/apps/
pbcs.dii/article?AID=/20070616/OPINION/706160305

Index

Page numbers for illustrations are in boldface.